Pioneers

TED TURNER

rourke biographies

Pioneers

TED TURNER

by
DAVID MARC FISCHER

1961

Rourke Publications, Inc.
Vero Beach, Florida 32964

∞ The paper used in this book conforms to the American
National Standard for Permanence of Paper for Printed
Library Materials, Z39.48-1984.

Library of Congress Cataloging-in-Publication Data
Fischer, David Marc, 1962-
 Ted Turner / written by David Marc Fischer.
  p. cm. — (Rourke biographies. Pioneers)
 Includes bibliographical references and index.
 Summary: A biography of the multimillionaire media
pioneer, creator of the Cable News Network, champion
yachtsman, and founder of environmental and humanitarian
organizations.
 ISBN 0-86625-496-X (alk. paper)
 1. Turner, Ted, 1938- —Juvenile literature. 2. Television broadcasting of news—United States—Juvenile literature. 3. Businessmen—United States—Biography— Juvenile literature. [1. Turner, Ted, 1938- . 2. Businessmen. 3. Television broadcasting of news.] I. Title. II.
Series.
PN4888.T4F57 1993
384.55'5'092—dc20
[B]   92-44761
                                                       CIP
                                                       AC

PRINTED IN THE UNITED STATES OF AMERICA

Contents

Color Illustrations

Chapter 1

Toward a Global Village

During the 1992 National League playoffs, television commentators occasionally turned away from the Atlanta Braves and Pittsburgh Pirates baseball teams to glance at three famous people sitting together in the stands. One was Jane Fonda, the Oscar-winning actress, political activist, and fitness advocate. Another was Jimmy Carter, the former president of the United States of America. The third person was Ted Turner, the owner of the Braves.

The slim, silver-haired Turner was not merely the owner of a baseball team. One of the wealthiest people in the world, he was truly a celebrity in his own right. Turner was a media pioneer, a billionaire adventurer who had built a fortune by exploiting many of the twentieth century's advances in transportation and communication. Recently married to Fonda, he had worked together with Carter for many years.

The Space Age

Born on November 19, 1938, Robert Edward (Ted) Turner grew up in the midst of a technological revolution. Cars, first mass-produced in 1903, were fast becoming an essential part of life in the United States, swiftly transporting people along a vast network of paved highways. Air travel was developing in ways only dreamed of in 1927, when Charles Lindbergh flew his propeller-driven airplane, *The Spirit of St. Louis*, across the Atlantic Ocean to Paris. The transition to jet and rocket engines during World War II (1939-1945) led to convenient airplane travel and supersonic flight. When, in 1957, the Soviet Union used supersonic speed to launch *Sputnik 1*, the first

9

TELEVISION TRANSMISSION

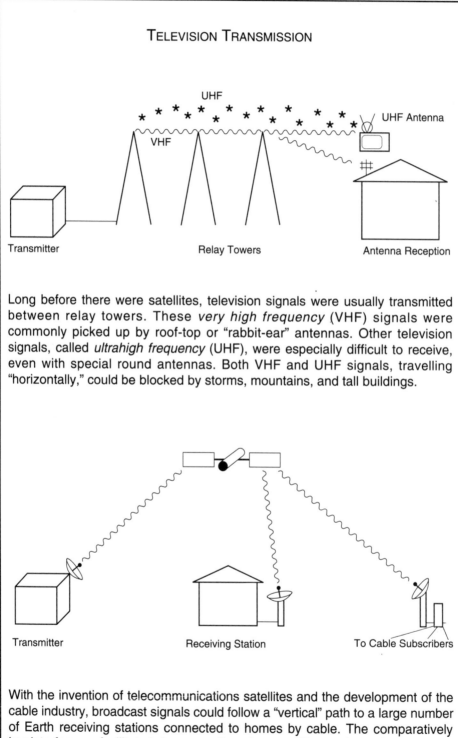

Long before there were satellites, television signals were usually transmitted between relay towers. These *very high frequency* (VHF) signals were commonly picked up by roof-top or "rabbit-ear" antennas. Other television signals, called *ultrahigh frequency* (UHF), were especially difficult to receive, even with special round antennas. Both VHF and UHF signals, travelling "horizontally," could be blocked by storms, mountains, and tall buildings.

With the invention of telecommunications satellites and the development of the cable industry, broadcast signals could follow a "vertical" path to a large number of Earth receiving stations connected to homes by cable. The comparatively low interference facilitated clear reception of many different channels.

Turner revealed his plan to take control of CBS at a press conference in New York.
(AP/Wide World Photos)

artificial satellite, into orbit around Earth, the human race entered the Space Age.

As fast, economical travel enabled more people to see more of the world, so did improvements in communications technology. The rise of television during Turner's youth ushered in a new age of electronic mass media. Before the development of broadcasting, people relied heavily on newspapers and magazines for information about current events. Now they could actually see and hear those events. In the summer of 1969, for example, an estimated one-fifth of the world's population witnessed a truly "giant leap for mankind" when astronaut Neil Armstrong set foot on the dry surface of the Moon. This achievement symbolized the interrelationship between modern mass communication and Space Age technology: Television and communications satellites had made it possible for a vast audience to observe historic events precisely as they were happening, wherever they were happening.

A Super Achiever

It takes many people to create and produce the sophisticated technology behind such transmissions. It also takes many dedicated and enthusiastic people to put such inventions to their best use. Ted Turner is one such visionary, a firm believer in the world-changing potential of mass communication in the Space Age.

While still a young man, Turner built a small fortune selling advertising space on billboards along Southern roadways. He also invested in a number of radio stations. In the 1970's, the entrepreneur began to make inroads in television, buying small stations in Georgia and North Carolina. By the end of the decade, he had transformed his Atlanta station into something he called his *SuperStation*, a "local" channel that used satellite and cable systems to transmit its programming all over the United States.

Once he had established the SuperStation, Turner began another project: the creation of a twenty-four-hour news channel. By 1982, he had established two news channels, the Cable News Network (CNN) and CNN2, which eventually became known as Headline News. The newscasts of CNN set the standard for a new era of television journalism. In only a few years, these networks were seen worldwide, by audiences with an unquenchable thirst to know more about their times. From pro-democracy demonstrations in the People's Republic of China (1989) to the Persian Gulf War (1991) to the arrival of military forces in Somalia (1992), Ted Turner's news networks enabled viewers to witness historical events as they happened. Although he was not the first to broadcast events "live," he was the first to do so on such a global scale.

By creating television stations to bring fast-breaking news events to viewers around the world, Ted Turner moved the planet one step closer to becoming a *global village*. This term, first used by Canadian media theorist Marshall McLuhan, describes a world in which electronic media act as extensions of the human senses of sight and hearing. This allows people to perceive events around the globe—and even in outer space—as easily as they observe the day-to-day occurrences in their immediate surroundings. Optimists like Turner believe that such technology will bring the peoples of the world closer together, so that, thinking of ourselves as neighbors in the same "global" village, we will become less likely to do things that hurt our earth or the people on it.

Turner's Space Age achievement is even more impressive considering his many other successes. As a competitive sailor, he has won numerous sailing events, including the 1977 America's Cup and the ill-fated Fastnet competition of 1979. As owner of the Atlanta Braves, he has seen his baseball team rise from the cellar to win National League pennants in 1991 and 1992. He also organized the 1986 and 1990 Goodwill Games, international events in which athletes from the United States and the Soviet Union (who, for political reasons, had not been allowed to face each other in the 1980 and 1984 Summer Olympic Games) could compete. Finally, he has established organizations, such as the Better World Society and the Turner Family Foundation, that are dedicated to improving the environment and fostering world peace.

A Fighting Spirit

Although Turner has celebrated many triumphs, he has also seen his share of disappointments. As a child, he suffered harsh and humiliating treatment at home and at school. While still a young man, he saw his sister die of a severe illness and his parents divorce. His misbehavior prevented him from graduating from college; later, as a yachtsman, his erratic actions in the public eye brought his business and marital problems to the attention of many. As a businessman, he took risks that at times made him a national laughingstock.

More than once, Turner seemed to be sailing toward ruin. Yet, by the time he had reached the age of fifty-four, Turner had surmounted these challenges. His businesses were thriving, and even his public behavior seemed to reflect personal growth.

The story of Ted Turner is the story of a man obsessed with proving himself not merely capable but superior in every project he undertakes. As he has put it:

> If any one thing is responsible for my success, it is that the minute I land on one plateau I immediately start trying to jump to the next one.[1]

Chapter 2

"Terrible" Ted

Ted Turner probably acquired most of his ambition and determination by following his father Ed's example. The son of a cotton farmer, Ed Turner had grown up in Sumner, Mississippi, near the Arkansas and Tennessee borders. Although financial obstacles forced him to leave North Carolina's Duke University without graduating, Ed was an industrious youth who switched to Mississippi State University, where he worked and studied his way to graduation.

After earning his diploma from "Ole Miss," Ed accepted a job in Memphis, Tennessee, with the General Outdoor Advertising Company, which was involved in selling billboard space along roadways. Eventually he went to work as a salesman for Queen City Chevrolet. On a business trip to Cincinnati, he met Florence Rooney, whose family owned the hotel where he was staying. His courtship of Florence revealed his single-mindedness. Despite the fact that she was dating someone else, Ed pursued her relentlessly until she agreed to marry him.

An Abusive Father

Only after marrying Ed did Florence discover her husband's worst qualities. He could be deceptive and manipulative: Although he had agreed to be married in a Catholic church, his intolerance of that faith necessitated the couple's switch to the Episcopalian church. He also drank too much alcohol. This habit would take its toll on the entire family.

The birth of son Ted and, later, daughter Mary Jane revealed Ed to be a demanding father. The elder Turner was a taskmaster who believed that frequent beatings would build his son's character. Florence was appalled by her husband's brutality.

In the face of his father's beatings, Ted might have become a fearful, timid child who hated Ed. That was not to be the case. Ted was a boy of strong and mixed emotions. Something of a prankster, he even took part in a nasty trick that Ed played on Florence. Once, she stood anxiously outside a locked room, listening to the familiar sound of Ed beating Ted. The door finally opened to reveal that her husband and son had faked the beating only to worry her.

Near the end of World War II, Ed took Florence and Mary Jane along with him on a Navy assignment but left young Ted behind at a Cincinnati boarding school. Ted, who hated being separated from his family, spent much of the next decade in such schools. Only after his father had purchased a billboard company in Savannah, Georgia, did Ted rejoin his family. From 1949 to 1950, he was able to take part in his family's daily life, hunting and fishing near home. He spent much of his time under the eye of Jimmy Brown, a trusted family employee.

During this time, Ted developed his sailing skills at the Savannah Yacht Club, where he raced against Carl Helfrich, the son of one of his father's friends. His aggressive, reckless maneuvers on the water caused him to capsize frequently, earning him the nickname Turnover Ted.

Shaping Up at McCallie

In 1950, Ed sent Ted off to school again—this time to a military academy, The McCallie School, in Chattanooga, Tennessee. Ted initially hated McCallie. Still very much a prankster, he rebelled, teasing teachers and regularly receiving disciplinary punishment. He became known as Terrible Ted. "At first, I was just a terrible cadet," he has recalled:

16

I did everything I could to rebel against the system, although I think I believed in it from the beginning. I was always having animals in my room and stuff like that, and getting into trouble one way or another, and then having to take the punishment like a man. I went through a lot, but it changed me, and after a while I shaped up. I wanted to be the best, and I saw that it could be done if you worked at it.[2]

Ted learned to love the green grass and red brick buildings of McCallie, participating in the school's Spanish Club and its boxing program, as well as the junior varsity football team. In the military program, he rose to the rank of captain and

Ted Turner as a cadet at the McCallie School. (Courtesy McCallie School)

received the title "Neatest Cadet" in his junior year. He also spent many fall and spring afternoons participating in the school's new sailing program at nearby Chickamauga Lake.

Not everything was smooth sailing during Ted's McCallie years. His sister Mary Jane was diagnosed as having severe lupus, a serious disease that left her vulnerable to other illnesses. An encephalitis attack resulted in brain damage that caused her to experience fits for eight years before her death in 1958. Years later, Ted would still be haunted by the memory of walking past her room: "I'd hear her banging her head against the wall in pain, screaming, 'God, let me die; God, let me die.'"[3]

Ted himself experienced a personal crisis in the mid-1950's. Despondent over a troubled relationship with a young woman, he contemplated committing suicide but managed to conquer those thoughts. During the summers, Ted returned home to find his father as demanding as ever: Ed had his son do maintenance work for the billboard company and charged him rent to live at home.

Ted Turns the Tables

During his senior year at McCallie, Ted surprised many with his dazzling performance as a debater. Although he had joined the debating team only that year, his argumentative skills and his aggressiveness enabled him to win a Tennessee state championship. His winning argument was in response to the following resolution: "Governmental subsidies should be granted according to need to high school graduates who qualify for additional training." Almost everyone who competed in the debate assumed that "need" referred to the neediness of financially disadvantaged students, but Ted realized that the word "need" could also refer to a government's need for well-trained citizens. He argued accordingly, flummoxing his opponent. In recognition of his resourcefulness, Ted received McCallie's Holton Harris Oratorical Medal.

As a secondary school student, Ted also showed tremendous discipline in preparing for his college board examinations. After scoring poorly on the verbal exam, he spent one summer expanding his vocabulary and boosted his score dramatically. Such scholastic achievement enabled him to attend one of the prestigious Ivy League colleges, Brown University, in Providence, Rhode Island. There he soon distinguished himself as an outstanding sailor, undefeated in his freshman year. One of his opponents was Will Sanders, whom Ted had known from Savannah. During the course of his enrollment at Brown, Ted served as both vice president of the debating union and commodore of the yacht club.

Suspension and Departure from Brown

Attending Brown did not tame Ted's wild side. Roger Vaughan, a classmate who became one of Ted's biographers, remembers him as a "spectacular" drinker, "likeable . . . despite his basic racist tendencies [and] his chauvinistic approach to women."[4] After Ed refused to let Ted accept a summer job with a yacht club, insisting that his son return to work with the billboard company, Ted really rebelled. His misbehavior at a nearby women's college earned him a suspension, which he spent in the Coast Guard. Upon his return to Brown, Ted declared his intention to major in classics. Learning of his son's plan, Ed wrote a letter that criticized Ted for his interest in Greek and Roman literature. Ted promptly submitted the letter to the student newspaper, which published it for all to read. Ed, who was in the midst of divorcing Florence, was angry and embarrassed at having his private letter exposed to public scrutiny.

Ted bowed to his father's will, changing his major to economics, but soon made trouble again, burning down his

Turner's crew carries him aloft after they have won America's Cup in 1977, the culmination of a lifelong love of sailing. (AP/Wide World Photos)

fraternity's homecoming display. Ted was finally compelled to leave Brown after he violated university rules by entertaining a woman in his dormitory room.

Broken Home, Battered Business

Ted left Brown with a buddy named Peter Dames. The two friends dreamed of sailing a boat across the Atlantic Ocean to Europe. When they arrived at the Turner plantation, they discovered that the boat had been damaged. Ted's family had also been broken: Ted's sister had died, and his parents had finally divorced.

Ted and Peter continued their travels together before parting ways in Florida. Peter ended up working with Ed Turner's company in Charleston, South Carolina; Ted fulfilled his obligation to the Coast Guard before accepting a job with

20

Turner Advertising Company in Macon, Georgia, in the fall of 1960.

In Macon, Ted appeared to settle down. He joined civic organizations and married Judy Nye, an excellent sailor whom he had met in 1958. As a husband-and-wife team, they then won a national championship. Like his father, however, Ted proved to be a domineering husband. He chose all of Judy's clothing and tightly controlled her spending. He insisted that she cook all the meals and buy only those breakfast cereals that appeared on Turner billboards. Tensions between them reached a breaking point after he used an extremely aggressive maneuver against her in a yacht race. Not long afterward, they were divorced. Although they tried to live together after the divorce, they finally decided that they and their children, Laura Lee and Robert Edward (Teddy) Turner IV, would be better off if the two of them lived apart.

Ted was clearly more successful in business. His years of work for his father had made him intimately familiar with the billboard industry. Together, Ed and Ted expanded the company until Ed was finally able to fulfill his dream of buying valuable Atlanta billboard properties.

There was a problem, however. In order to complete the purchase agreement, Ed had placed his company on very unsure financial footing. Now, to raise the money to keep the company alive, Ed believed that he had to give up his newly acquired Atlanta business. Although Ted strenuously tried to convince his father not to do so, Ed, increasingly distraught, sold it to a business partner, Bob Naegele. The circumstances surrounding this reversal troubled Ed so deeply that six months later, on March 5, 1963, he killed himself with a pistol.

Ted had lost Mary Jane to disease and Judy to a divorce. Now he had lost his father, and it seemed as though he might lose the business his father had spent a lifetime building.

Chapter 3

Birth of an Empire

Shocked by his father's suicide, Ted Turner was also outraged that the Atlanta billboard company, which he expected to inherit, had just been sold. He immediately decided to use all of his resources to wrest it back from Bob Naegele. With two weeks to spare before the selling process was completed, Turner pursued his goal aggressively. He hired some of the company's staff members as his own employees and had them transfer the Atlanta properties to his control. He also threatened to start a rival company that would erect billboards in front of Naegele's.

Turner knew that this strategy might ruin him as well as Naegele, but he correctly sensed that his opponent would be unwilling to engage in any battles. Naegele and his associates began to negotiate, offering to sell the company back for $200,000. Turner agreed, although he was unsure of where he could find the money. Then he proposed a stock plan: If Naegele and his group invested the $200,000 themselves, they could share in the company's future profits. After all the wheeling and dealing was over, Turner had achieved his objective: He retained the billboard business as President and Chief Operating Officer of the Turner Advertising Company.

A Second Marriage

In the following years, Turner expanded the outdoor advertising business while engaging in other pursuits. His old buddy from Brown University, Peter Dames, introduced him to Janie Smith, an airline attendant from Birmingham, Alabama. As his father had pursued Florence, Ted wooed Janie relentlessly, telephoning her during the day and picking her up in his Ferrari sports car at night. They were married on June 2, 1964; about six months later, Laura Lee and Teddy moved in with them. Although Ted could still be a harshly demanding husband, lecturing Janie about stocking the refrigerator and managing the laundry, this second marriage was far more stable than the first. Over the years, the family expanded with the births of Rhett, Beauregard, and Sarah Jean.

Sailing Onward

Turner spent much time away from his family. When he was not away at work, he was often sailing. Only months after his father's death, he became the first and only person to win the Atlanta Yacht Club championships in both the Y-Flier and Flying Dutchman fleets. Despite such victories, he also experienced some spectacular defeats as he ventured into races involving larger boats. In 1964 he chartered a forty-foot vessel, *Scylla*, for the Montego Bay Race from Florida to Jamaica.

Just bringing *Scylla* from New York to Miami was nearly disastrous: A fire broke out on board, the ship almost sank when pumps malfunctioned, food and water ran low, and the crew even got lost and ran aground before arriving. The race itself extended this series of mishaps, until Turner finally gave up and brought his hungry, disoriented sailing party into port in the Bahamas, having failed to travel even half the distance to the finish line. Tenacious as ever, he refused to let the loss discourage him. He entered competition after competition, sometimes with his old mentor Jimmy Brown on his crew, finishing first in his class in the 1966 Transatlantic Race and even winning the Montego Bay Race sailing *Vamoose* in 1967.

Exploring New Opportunities

Around the time Turner achieved these sailing victories, he was anxious to expand his business ventures beyond

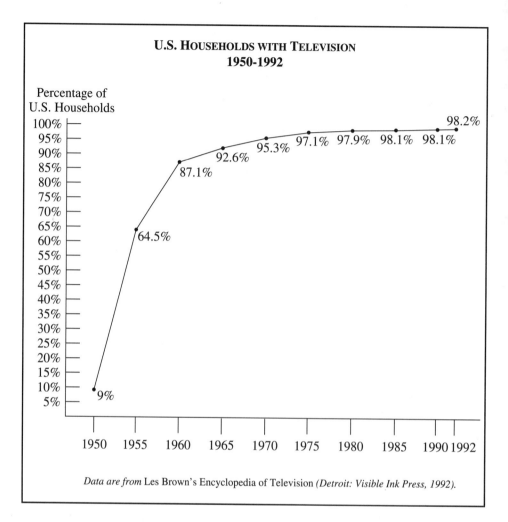

U.S. HOUSEHOLDS WITH TELEVISION
1950-1992

Percentage of
U.S. Households

100%
95%
90%
85%
80%
75%
70%
65%
60%
55%
50%
45%
40%
35%
30%
25%
20%
15%
10%
5%

9%
64.5%
87.1%
92.6%
95.3%
97.1%
97.9%
98.1%
98.1%
98.2%

1950 1955 1960 1965 1970 1975 1980 1985 1990 1992

Data are from Les Brown's Encyclopedia of Television *(Detroit: Visible Ink Press, 1992).*

billboards. He invested in PlasTrend, an innovator in sailboat design. He also formed Turner Communications Corporation to explore opportunities in outdoor advertising, radio, and television. With two associates, he visited Chattanooga to consider buying a failing radio station there. Soon after their departure, the three decided to go ahead with the purchase. Yet, when they contacted the sellers, they found that they had been too slow: The station had just been sold. Having learned a lesson about speed in business decisions, Turner decided to buy the station anyway, at a much higher cost, from its new owner.

Turner set about improving the station with his usual focus and determination. When he bought it, it offered only the dullest programming, including live golf coverage. Turner brought in professional announcers and changed the programming to a "top-forty" format. He promoted the station by using billboard space that he had not been able to sell to other advertisers. Just as he had continued the expansion of his outdoor advertising business throughout the South, buying the billboard business owned by his old sailing rival Will Sanders' family, Turner began to buy and merge with other broadcast companies in South Carolina and Florida.

Turner Turns to Television

In 1970, the year Turner hired Sanders as his vice president of finance, Ted extended his business activities to television. Sensing the great advertising potential of the medium, Turner merged Turner Communications Corporation with Rice Broadcasting at a cost of $3 million, gaining control of Atlanta's struggling Channel 17, a UHF station that was losing $50,000 a month. Turner was barely able to win the support of his stockholders to make this risky investment. Yet he was so sure that even small UHF stations offered great opportunities for raising advertising revenue that six months later he used his own money to buy Channel 36, a Charlotte, North Carolina, station that was losing $30,000 a month.

Together with Sanders, sales manager Gerry Hogan, special projects executive Terence McGuirk, corporate controller Paul Beckham, and chief engineer Eugene Wright, Turner threw himself into the broadcasting business with the same zeal he had applied to building his billboard and radio businesses. In Charlotte, he went on the air to raise $35,000 from viewers. To raise more money, he sold the struggling PlasTrend, as well as the billboard businesses in Macon, Charleston, Columbus, and Richmond. He insisted that his television stations spend as little money as possible, instructing employees to tape commercials over old tapes rather than buy new ones.

At first, Channel 17—named WTCG in recognition of the company's new name, Turner Communications Group—was plagued with technical difficulties. Once, after the transmission line blew, it had to go off the air for a whole week. On another occasion, the broadcast of a movie had to be canceled when it appeared upside-down. Despite these difficulties, Turner found many ways to show that his first television station, which was sometimes derided as "number seven in a five-station market,"[5] was still a competitor. When a rival station suddenly went off the air in 1971, Turner threw a televised "Thank You, Atlanta" party to celebrate his station's "advance" to number four in a four-station market.

To coax viewers away from the competition, Turner thought hard about programming. On Sunday mornings, when the other channels were broadcasting religious shows, he offered films on *Academy Awards Theater*, which he sometimes hosted. During the dinner hour, when the other channels offered news, he broadcast reruns of the original *Star Trek*. He restricted the forty minutes of news required by the Federal Communications Commission (FCC) to the early-morning hours, showed professional wrestling matches, and built a library of old movies and television shows, scheduling reruns of such popular classics as *I Love Lucy*, *Gilligan's Island*, *Leave It to Beaver*, *Petticoat Junction*, *Father Knows Best*, *The Andy Griffith Show*, and *Gomer Pyle, USMC*.

Turner's main competition came from the "Big Three" networks—ABC, NBC, and CBS—which offered popular original programs to their "affiliate" stations in Atlanta. When the NBC affiliate chose not to buy five network shows, Turner took the opportunity to purchase and show them instead, his billboards brashly announcing "The NBC Network Moves to Channel 17." Perhaps his most audacious move against the NBC affiliate took place when he bought the rights to broadcast Atlanta Braves games for five years. Even though, according to former Braves publicist Bob Hope (not the famous comedian), "there wasn't a soul in Atlanta who would admit to ever having watched Channel 17,"[6] the team's main office could hardly resist Turner's $2.5 million offer—in the past, it had actually *paid* the NBC affiliate to broadcast the games.

Hope, who had regarded Channel 17 as "a Mickey Mouse station with a reputation of showing only cartoons, old grade-D movies, and 1950s television reruns,"[7] soon found himself and the rest of Atlanta obeying the message in WTCG's slogan: Watch This Channel Grow. By 1973, Channel 17 had begun to make money; Channel 36 took a bit longer.

Growth was an important component of Turner's business strategy. It was not enough for his stations to make profits: Turner wanted them to attract ever-increasing audiences and advertising revenues. In Atlanta he put his rhetorical skills to good use, appealing to potential advertisers with persuasive sales presentations, offering answers for every question they posed with a combination of physical gesture and almost incessant chatter. When potential clients criticized his programming for being mainly black-and-white, he argued that it would make their color commercials stand out more. When they complained that his audience was small, he bragged that, though few in number, the viewers were a perfect consumer audience: wealthy and intelligent. How else could they afford televisions with UHF reception and figure out how to use them?

A Fourth Network?

Ted's aggressiveness increased the value of Turner Communications Group and established him as a growing force in the media. His influence and reputation reached an even higher plateau in the mid-1970's, when he transformed WTCG, which once had a broadcast range of only forty-five miles, into WTBS, a "superstation" viewable over ten million square miles.

Turner had long sought ways to distribute his signal to more viewers and thereby charge advertisers more money for time on his station. He saw his chance in 1975, when he found a way to take advantage of space technology and changing government regulations to broadcast his signal nationwide using a satellite. Such a plan would not only increase audience size but improve reception as well. Although no independent station had ever chosen to broadcast via satellite before, Turner

Turner presses a big button to "start" the Cable Music Channel—one of many broadcasting enterprises—in 1984. (AP/Wide World Photos)

saw that it could be done. The growing industry of cable operators would be able to pick up his signal on satellite dishes and deliver it to subscribers' homes.

Turner acted quickly. First he had to obtain an earthbound station to exchange signals with the satellite. Establishing one near his studios in Atlanta, he formed a company, Southern Satellite Systems (SSS), to operate and distribute his signal. When lawyers told him that regulations prevented him from owning the earth station, he sold SSS for the token amount of one dollar and went ahead with his plan, assured that he would still be able to use the facilities.

On January 3, 1976, Turner made another important move: He secured valuable rights to broadcast future Atlanta Braves games by buying the team for $10 million. He even used the club's own money to make the first payment.

Because the SuperStation could be seen across the country, it appeared to be a triple threat to the Big Three networks and their affiliates. It could steal viewers away from network programs, reduce network advertising revenue, and make cable television more attractive to advertisers. In many ways, the SuperStation was the ultimate nightmare of the Big Three: a Fourth Network that would undermine their near-monopoly over the medium of television. Speaking before a congressional subcommittee on the future of cable television, Turner embraced the role of the Big Three's biggest threat:

I would love [Channel 17] to become a superstation. I would love desperately to create a Fourth Network for cable television, producing our own programs, not just running *I Love Lucy* and *Gilligan's Island* for the fifty-seventh time. And I intend to go that way, if we are allowed to.

You have to remember that there are three supernetworks who only own four or five stations apiece that are controlling the way this nation thinks and raking off exorbitant profits, and most of [the] local

stations that everybody is crying about are just [affiliates] carrying . . .
network programs. . . .

So if we do become super, it will be another voice. Perhaps it might
be a little more representative of what we think the average American
would like to see. A little less blood and gore on television and more
sports and old movies and that sort of thing. . . . [8]

By the end of 1976, WTCG, the nation's most profitable
UHF station, had become "The SuperStation That Serves the
Nation," available to cable subscribers across the United States
and seen in nearly 700,000 households. Soon thereafter, to
secure more sports programming, Turner bought a controlling
interest in the Atlanta Hawks basketball team and obtained the
rights to telecast many other Atlanta sporting events.

Over a fifteen-year period, Turner had saved a troubled
regional billboard business and built a national media empire
by investing in struggling radio, television, and sports
enterprises. By the end of 1979, his SuperStation (renamed
WTBS) was seen by 8.9 million households and was the
flagship of Turner's media corporation, now renamed Turner
Broadcasting System (TBS). The three networks were eyeing
him as a serious competitor: He had financial strength, a
growing national audience, control over access to sports in
Atlanta, and a sizable library of old and popular movies and
television programs. In a 1978 interview, Turner was able to
gloat over his accomplishments and chortle over their fears.

Can you imagine that? A little old raggedy station with a hundred
employees and a bunch of torn-up furniture is going to destroy
television and cause the motion-picture industry to collapse![9]

Engineering the rise of his SuperStation, Turner had become a
serious challenger to the Big Three.

Chapter 4

The Mouth from the South

When Turner purchased the Atlanta Braves in 1976, nobody involved with the team knew what to expect from the television tycoon. He assumed command upon his arrival, telling employees that they would have to work harder than they had ever worked before and ordering them to start the business day half an hour earlier, at 8:30 A. M.

He plunged ahead over the coming months, attracting attention with his brash decisions. Knowing little about baseball, Turner familiarized himself with the game by visiting spring training with the trusted Terence McGuirk. In April, he signed pitching sensation Andy Messersmith, one of baseball's first free agents, to a million-dollar contract.

Early in his reign as owner, Turner seized the opportunity to sign baseball great Hank Aaron as Player Development Director, a position that Aaron held from 1977 until he became vice president of the ball club in 1990. Turner also appointed the slugger to the board of TBS. Aaron, who had just completed a sterling career on the field, welcomed the chance to prove his worth behind the scenes. "Ted Turner was the best thing that could have happened to me," he reflected in his autobiography.[10]

Turner invited criticism when he fired popular Braves traveling secretary Donald Davidson. One of the best-loved personalities in baseball, Davidson had broken rules preventing employees from flying first-class, riding in limousines, and staying in hotel suites. Critics of Turner felt that the punishment was harsh and mean-spirited. Wrote Frank Hyland in the *Atlanta Journal*:

31

Ted Turner has a lot of money. Ted Turner has enthusiasm. Ted Turner has his own baseball team. Ted Turner belongs to some of the world's most prestigious clubs. But Ted Turner has no class.[11]

Years later, Aaron still felt that firing Davidson was the worst mistake Turner had ever made.

A Winner for "Losersville"

Turner told publicist Bob Hope that he intended the publicity surrounding his activities to make him the "most famous man on earth next to Muhammad Ali."[12] With Hope's help, Turner planned to use that kind of attention to inject fun and excitement into the city known in the sports world as "Losersville, USA." If the Braves could not win, at least they could work on bringing fans to the ballpark. "I want this team to be like McDonald's," Turner told Hope. "I want an atmosphere built here that will make kids want to come to the games. I want it to be exciting."[13]

Exciting it was. It was also silly, sassy, and sometimes stupefying. At the team's opening home game, Turner inaugurated the season by leading the large but not sold-out crowd in a rendition of "Take Me Out to the Ball Game." In the following months and years he was a common sight at the stadium, which he dubbed his "big playpen." Instead of sitting in a private box, he reserved seats at field level, where he could chew tobacco, drink beer, greet fans, sign autographs, address the stadium using a newly installed microphone, and even jump onto the field to congratulate home-run hitters or cavort with mascots like Susie Sweeper and the Bleacher Creature. He modernized the stadium with television monitors and a scoreboard that displayed instant replays.

Like other ballparks, Atlanta-Fulton County Stadium hosted a Bat Day, Cap Day, T-Shirt Day, Old-Timers Game, Banner Day, and Poster Day. Other events, such as a Blind Date

Night, distinguished the home of the Braves. On the day of
Andy Messersmith's debut, the field was the site of a wild
post-game Easter egg hunt. Over the years, it also
accommodated a frog-jumping contest, spaghetti and pizza
dinners, a controversial wet T-shirt contest, and a baseball

Ted Turner, new owner of the Atlanta Braves. (AP/Wide World Photos)

game pitting twins against each other. Wedlock and Headlock
Day featured on-the-field weddings and wrestling. On
Diamond Night, women received a piece of jewelry; six had
the chance to dive into a small haystack to dig for a diamond
inside it. On Mattress-Stacking Night, Turner joined fraternity
and sorority members competing to see how many people
could be stacked on a mattress in one minute. During the
$25,000 Cash Scramble, fans had ninety seconds to pick up as
many dollar bills as they could.

A circus atmosphere prevailed at the ballpark. There were fireworks, laser light shows, and stunts galore. A local disk jockey leapt into a giant ice cream sundae, almost drowning in the process. The Great Wallenda walked on a wire stretched across the top of the stadium, and a gentleman known as The Human Bomb appeared to survive blowing himself up. Turner himself participated in numerous competitions staged on the field: He bloodied his face outracing ace reliever Tug McGraw in an event called the Baseball Nose Push; he lost to Frank Hyland in an ostrich race; and he emerged victorious in a Motorized Bathtub race.

One night Turner promised a sparse crowd of spectators that they could come back free-of-charge the following night if the Braves lost. He kept his vow when the team lost.

Braves manager Dave Bristol often disagreed with the way Turner behaved but admired his spirit. The players, who nicknamed their owner Teddy Ballgame, were puzzled by the unusually personable owner who showered, hunted, and played poker with them.

Although the Braves continued to lose, Ted's publicity campaign seemed to have its intended effect: 1976 attendance was nearly twice that of 1975, and the stadium was sold out for the 1977 opening game. Turner and Hope brought their promotional abilities to the Hawks as well, at times hardly seeming to care if the team would ever improve. "The Hawks are so bad *I* was going to play,"[14] Turner once joked. Basketball crowds at the Omni Arena were, at various times, treated to an indoor fireworks display that blew holes in the roof, comic routines staged in the audience, and post-game rock concerts.

The Braves would not improve markedly for some years, but Turner's touch somehow seemed to have had a positive effect on the Hawks. By the end of the 1978 season, the team had reached the playoffs with a .500 record, and Hubie Brown, who had been responsible for player selection, had been voted Coach of the Year by the National Basketball Association.

Hero or Madman?

After Ted took over the Braves and the Hawks, his life was more frantic than ever. Typically, when he was not dashing off to yachting competitions, he would deliver a speech at breakfast, sell advertising time the rest of the morning, deliver another speech at lunch, conduct Braves business in the afternoon, and attend games in the evening. He could be a confusing boss. One day he might insult or event fire an employee; then, after days had passed, he would explain that he had been joking. Once he warned staff members that he would be watching them closely for a week. At the follow-up meeting, he began to recite the National Anthem with a baseball bat in his hands. After making a few reassuring remarks he banged the bat on a table and ended the meeting.

Turner's behavior as owner of the Braves and Hawks bolstered his reputation as a maverick. To many in Atlanta he was a folk hero, greeted by strangers virtually everywhere he went. To others, however—including the baseball commissioner's office—he was the crude Mouth from the South.

The reputation was not merely the result of his antics—not that he might jump on the field after his players hit home runs, or, on his early television advertisements for the Braves, comically call himself "the frightened new owner of the Atlanta Braves."[15] Rather, the controversy revolved around some more questionable practices: for example, his tendency to test the league's bylaws of conduct by giving players monetary incentives to play well, or attempting to nickname Messersmith "Channel" and give him the number 17.

Turner finally went too far when he defied league rules by expressing his interest in acquiring Gary Matthews before the

Though the Braves had trouble scoring victories, the fans—and Turner—had fun. (AP/Wide World Photos)

outfielder's contract with the Giants had expired. As a result, on January 18, 1977, Baseball Commissioner Bowie Kuhn denied the Braves their first-round draft choice and suspended Turner for one year. Turner was reinstated while he challenged this decision in court, but he was suspended again when he tried to make himself the Braves' manager on May 11.

Throughout the dispute, Turner continued to antagonize the commissioner. Report after report described the unsettling behavior of the Mouth from the South as he barked in public, threatened to punch Kuhn's attorney, and even talked about shooting the commissioner himself.[16]

Although he disliked being known as the Mouth from the South, Turner was glad to attract so much publicity. When he was suspended, almost forty thousand admirers signed a petition on his behalf. "I'm the most colorful guy around," he boasted.[17] What his fans might not have realized was that Turner had a motive for his obnoxious behavior. In 1977 he wanted to race in one of the world's most prestigious yachting events. Realizing that suspension from the league would free him to concentrate on that competition while boosting his status as a folk hero, he had deliberately invited the punishment. Only after his advisers informed him that he had carried the act too far did he stop. The draft choice was reinstated, but the suspension was upheld.

Chapter 5

Captain Outrageous

While Turner was busy building his SuperStation, promoting his sports teams, and overseeing his other business operations, he also competed in many sailing events around the globe. The man who had applied his Midas touch to outdoor advertising, radio, and television had also, according to champion sailor Dennis Conner, become "famous for his ability to get the very best out of his sometimes-outdated boats using a steady crew of old friends."[18]

Turner sometimes met with disappointment: In 1968 he failed to qualify in the Olympic yachting trials. Yet, despite being distracted by his various enterprises, he was accomplished enough to be designated Yachtsman of the Year by the United States Yacht Racing Union in both 1970 and 1973. By 1974, Turner felt ready to compete in the defense trials of the America's Cup competition.

The America's Cup

One of the most famous yachting competitions in the world, the triennial America's Cup originated in 1851, when the New York Yacht Club first challenged others to compete for its coveted silver trophy. While attending Brown University, Turner had witnessed part of the prestigious America's Cup race and had begun to dream about participating in it himself.

All yacht races require successful teamwork. A syndicate of wealthy backers selects a manager, a designer, and a builder, as well as a skipper who oversees a crew. For his first America's Cup competition, in Newport, Rhode Island, Turner skippered a radically designed boat, *Mariner*, but problems with the yacht and the syndicate prevented it from getting far in the competition. By August, Turner had been fired from the helm, replaced by his tactician, Conner, who lost all four of his races.

Discouraged but not yet defeated, Turner tried to retain his fighting spirit. "Getting axed . . . was the best thing that could happen to me," he later recalled, "because it was an opportunity to show I could function under adverse circumstances."[19] Conner was left with the same impression: "*Mariner* was not a fun experience—under-financed and under-managed," he recalled. "Turner was great, but he didn't know what he was doing, not really; it was a learning experience for him."[20] Instead of giving up, Turner switched to skipper an even slower vessel, *Valiant,* and surprised no one when he failed to reach the finals, which were won by sailmaker Ted Hood on his yacht *Challenger.*

Turner and Sally Lindsay beam over their trophies after being named Yachtsman and Yachtswoman of 1973. (AP/Wide World Photos)

Learning from Defeat

By the time Turner returned to Newport in 1977, he was
notorious as the Mouth from the South, the television and
sports maverick who had just been suspended from baseball.
Although Turner was known in the business world as brash
and aggressive, it was as a skipper that he was most
intimidating. For years he had been known as an intense
competitor whose credos were "I'd rather sink than lose"[21] and
"Either lead, follow, or get out of the way!"[22]

Notwithstanding Turner's reputation, the sailors in Newport
noticed that, on the water, he appeared to have learned some
important lessons since his previous attempt. Three more years
of experience and hard work had enabled him to build his
confidence and put racing in its proper perspective.

His return to Newport also reflected better planning. After
being named skipper of Hood's old boat, *Courageous*, he
joined the New York Yacht Club to increase his chance of
raising crucial funds. Resistance to his membership and
participation was everywhere; even his own syndicate
manager, Alfred Lee Loomis, Jr., did not want him to win.
Loomis focused his hopes on his other boat, *Independence*,
skippered by Hood. "I wanted someone to put together an
independent organization that would force Hood to do his very
best," Loomis said.[23]

The Winning Spirit

Turner bridled at the thought of being a mere pacer for
Hood. As he saw it, he was investing much of his own money
and effort in a race that Loomis wanted to turn into a training
session. Heated arguments erupted over this disagreement.
Loomis wanted Turner to use only Hood's sails; Turner
wanted to choose his own combination of sails from Hood and
another competitor, Lowell North from California. North
finally put an end to the dispute by refusing to sell sails to

Son Rhett, eleven, helps Turner sand the boom of Courageous. (AP/Wide World Photos)

Turner. Turner concluded that—with an older boat, restrictions on the sails he could use, and the hostility he received from other members of the yachting establishment—he could count on only himself and his crew to make *Courageous* a winner.

Although Ted's crew was younger than others in the competition, its members were carefully chosen. "I did the best I could at putting together the most mature and experienced crew I possibly could," he recalled.[24] Dressed in blue, green, and white, the crew members included his longtime sailing partner Carl Helfrich and tactician Gary Jobson, who had been named College Sailor of the Year in 1972 and 1973. Turner thought of his team as underdogs, unwelcomed by the New York Yacht Club and even his own syndicate manager. "We need to win because we're just a bunch of bums," he announced to his crew.[25] It was fitting that the theme song from the film *Rocky*, "Gonna Fly Now," became the theme song of the *Courageous*. In recognition of his fighting spirit, some began calling Ted "Captain Courageous."

The Rise of Captain Outrageous

As the competition progressed, Ted's wild side kept rising to the surface. Swaggering around Newport in his Southern Railway engineer's cap, he bitterly needled North for not selling him sails and sometimes berated his own crew members to get them in shape. Once, he saw a man wearing a "Beat the Mouth" button at a restaurant. Turner ripped the button off, flung it aside, and showered the man with insults. After misbehaving at a midsummer party, Turner apologized in writing, admitting that he had drunk too much alcohol.[26]

For relaxation, Turner watched the Braves on Channel 17, using an earth receiving station that he had brought to Newport, and entertained the players when they came to visit. Although the Braves had the fourth highest payroll in baseball, the players lost regularly during Turner's suspension, amassing the team's worst record since 1935 and attracting the second lowest attendance in the major leagues. Turner wondered if the team was losing because he was devoting so much effort to the America's Cup.

In July's early races *Courageous* suffered some losses but put together an outstanding series of wins after the crew acquired new sails and practiced changing them. As the competition progressed, Hood and *Independence* were eliminated, but many still thought that another boat, North's *Enterprise*, would prevail. In August, however, North was fired after *Enterprise*'s performance failed to meet expectations.

Before his final race against *Enterprise* and its new skipper, Turner cockily taunted crew members of the 1977 challenger, *Australia*, by pulling his boat alongside theirs and leading his crew in a chorus of "Waltzing Matilda," the unofficial anthem of Australia. At the starting line, he offered a grand salute to the selection committee, then proceeded to qualify as finalist. Still in a singing mood after the selection party, Turner bid farewell to the *Enterprise* crew by leading some *Courageous* crew members in a rendition of "California, Here I Come."

Before facing *Australia* in the finals, Turner kept himself well occupied, competing in another local race, keeping up with the Braves, and celebrating the signing of the Panama Canal Treaty with a fellow Georgian, President Jimmy Carter, at a state dinner in Washington, D.C.

A Hero Scores a Zero

A flotilla of seacraft—as well as planes, helicopters, and a Goodyear blimp—congregated around Newport for the final days of the America's Cup competition. The *Courageous* team successfully defended the cup with four straight wins over *Australia*, but Turner's post-race behavior threatened to overshadow the victory.

As *Courageous* returned to port, Turner stood triumphant, bare-chested, a cigar in his mouth, arms held aloft in a *V*. By the time he arrived at the last press conference, he was carrying two bottles of liquor, which Channel 17 general manager Sid Pike tried to hide under a table. Pike tensely looked on as Turner and Jobson lit cigars and the Australians sang "Dixie" in their honor. Soon Turner, loudly deriding Pike, reached under the table for the liquor. In front of a battery of photographers and reporters, he tossed back drinks, heckled other speakers, and muddled through a speech of his own before his crew carried him out.

Captured on film, this embarrassing behavior of Captain Outrageous was seen widely, not to be forgotten for years to come.[27] Yet Turner's admirers would also remember his impressive comeback from the poor showing in 1974. By the end of 1977, the triumph of Captain Courageous had been celebrated throughout the media, earning him an unprecedented third designation as Yachtsman of the Year.

Racing to Fastnet

After his America's Cup victory, Turner set his sights on one more competition in which he could prove his abilities. In a book he and Jobson wrote after their victory on *Courageous*, he mentioned that there was a race even more competitive than the America's Cup: Fastnet, at Plymouth, England, on the Irish Sea. For a week in August, 1979, the two men sailed on *Tenacious* with a crew that included Ted's sixteen-year-old son Teddy.

There were a series of races at Fastnet. In the first race, to France and back, Turner drilled his crew members into shape. When calm weather slowed to a virtual halt, Turner relentlessly exploited every breeze to keep the boat moving, earning the first-place standing in the yacht's class. As the week continued, the crew worked with greater precision,

Turner responds to cheers for luck as Courageous *heads out to Rhode Island Sound in her race against* Australia. (AP/Wide World Photos)

winning the Brittania Cup and the New York Yacht Club Challenge Cup.

The final course, to Fastnet Rock and back, was notorious for its strong currents and unpredictable breezes. These conditions could make sailing both difficult and dangerous. On the first day of the event, Turner and his crew worked their way through the flotilla of 303 boats, trying to obtain a good position. Many of the yachts tried to follow *Tenacious* and two other ships through rough coastal waters but became stuck in tricky currents.

For two days, *Tenacious* sailed on, obtaining a leading position as crew members worked in four-hour shifts, changing sails regularly to take full advantage of the wind and even relaxing over delicious meals. Their routine was soon shattered, however, as they began their return trip. Radio reports warned that severe gales were on the way.

Sailing in Stormy Seas

The storm struck after sunset. Rainfall and strong winds intensified through the night, forcing crew members to fasten onto the windward rail with safety harnesses. By midnight they learned that they were facing Force 10 (hurricane) winds. Shouting for the crew to take down the mainsail, Turner took over the helm. Water crashed over the deck as waves twenty-five feet high shook *Tenacious*.

Fastnet became a nightmare as powerful winds hurled the yacht through a tunnel of curling waves. Teddy and other crew members became violently ill, their throats parched by salty spray. Their fear doubled as, speeding into the night, they glimpsed twinkling lights dead ahead: the distress signals of the yachts they had left behind earlier in the race. Those yachts were also out of control. *Tenacious* sped into their midst, bucking violently and threatening to ram them.

Over the radio, Turner began to hear distress calls and

reports of helicopter searches for the endangered vessels and crew members. As *Tenacious* sped ahead with Jim Mattingly at the helm, Turner and navigator Peter Bowker desperately tried to plot a course. Neglecting to wear a harness, Bowker was flung across the deck, bending the steering wheel and losing his radio direction finder. That forced Turner to guide *Tenacious* clear of the treacherous Scilly Isles, which lay between them and Plymouth.

When the sun finally rose, crew members watched the yacht hurtle over thirty-foot towers of water and slam down slopes of white foam. After nervously scanning the horizon for the truly lethal waves, twice as high, that are found in such rough seas, they were relieved when, around noontime, Turner announced that the storm had subsided.

A Troubled Homecoming

When *Tenacious* crossed the finish line at 10:30 P.M., the crew began to learn just how disastrous Fastnet had been. The grim atmosphere in Plymouth completely contrasted with the boisterous revelry that had followed the 1977 America's Cup competition in Newport. Of the 303 boats that had started the final race at Fastnet, only ninety had finished. Five had sunk, and twenty others had been abandoned. Worst of all, nineteen participants had died in the storm-tossed seas.

Turner, who himself had been reported "lost at sea," shocked many when he attempted to celebrate his crew's win. Although he could not help but be moved by the tragedy, he sounded harsh as he criticized many of his competitors' boats as not being as sturdy and seaworthy as his. "We won because we had a good crew and a strong boat and a lot of experience, and the people who didn't have those went to the big regatta in the sky," he said. "I'm not going to say I'm sorry I won."[28]

Chapter 6

Chicken Noodle News

Although Turner earned an outstanding victory at Fastnet, his post-race behavior again seemed to overshadow his triumph. Soon, however, Captain Outrageous vanished from the yacht racing scene. After being designated the 1979 Yachtsman of the Year but failing to reach the finals in the 1980 America's Cup competition (winner Dennis Conner's team had invested $2 million compared to Turner's $600,000), he put *Courageous* up for sale. In June, 1981, he announced his retirement from ocean racing.

By that time, Turner was also delegating some of his authority over the Braves and Hawks. Rather than engage in more wild publicity stunts and yachting events, he was channeling his energies into a different kind of sport: the race to create the first successful all-news cable network.

The Cable News Concept

The thought of Ted Turner involving himself in television journalism was surprising to everyone who knew him, for he had always claimed to hate news. In fact, in the mid-1970's, when veteran television newsman Reese Schonfeld approached Channel 17's general manager, Sid Pike, about developing news programming, Pike laughed him out of his office. At that time, anyone who was awake to watch Channel 17 news at 3:00 A.M. knew that the station's news program was a joke: It featured anchorman Bill Tush, who was known to deliver the news with a picture of the distinguished anchorman Walter Cronkite in front of his face, and a character named the Unknown Newsman, who reported with a bag over his head.

1. 1977: America's Cup victor. (Robert Azzi/Woodfin Camp)

2. Turner at a Braves game: always doing more than one thing at a time. (Jim
   Richardson/Woodfin Camp)

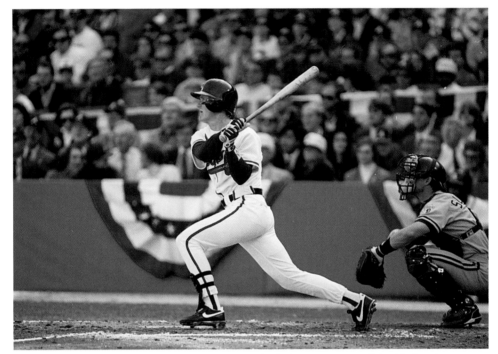

3. Atlanta Braves batter Jeff Blauser blasts a triple during game two of the National League Championship series, 1992. (AP/Wide World Photos)

4. Turner applauds his team. (Jim Richardson/Woodfin Camp)

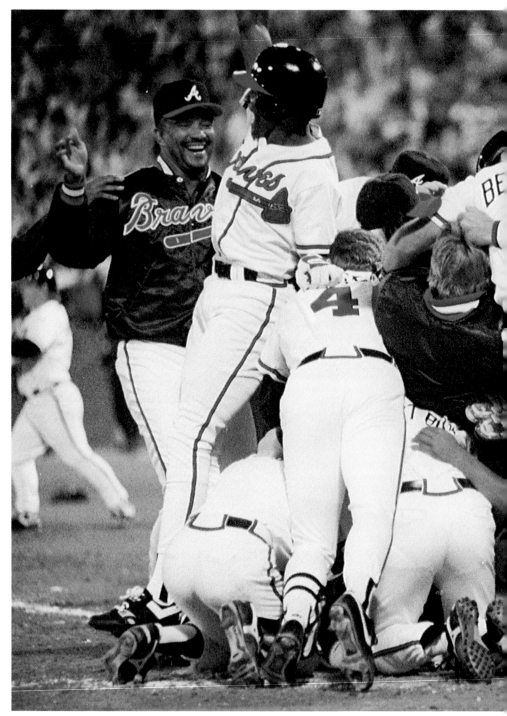

5. The Braves' Otis Nixon leaps into the air as teammates pile on Sid Bream, who scored the run that won Atlanta the National League Pennant for 1992. (AP/Wide World Photos)

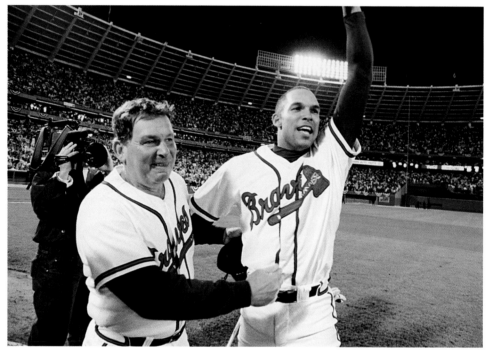

6. The Braves' Dave Justice (right) celebrates with manager Bobby Cox after winning
   the National League Pennant and the right to play in 1992's World Series. (AP/Wide
   World Photos)

7. Turner at CNN's studio in Atlanta, Georgia. (AP/Wide World Photos)

8. CNN's world headquarters newsroom in Atlanta, Georgia. (Jeff Greenberg/
   Unicorn Stock Photos)

9. CNN's coverage of the Persian Gulf War brought history-making events into our living
   rooms as they happened. (AP/Wide World Photos)

10. Turner and Fonda at the Better World Society awards dinner in New York City. (AP/
   Wide World Photos)

11. Turner and Jane Fonda were married on December 21, 1991, at the couple's ranch in northern Florida. (AP/Wide World Photos)

12. Their marriage was the event of the season and marked not only the commitment vows of two dynamic people but also the union of two media giants. Pictured from left to right: Peter Fonda, Troy (Jane's son), Shirlee Fonda (Henry Fonda's widow), the bride and groom. (AP/Wide World Photos)

Sometimes a German shepherd wearing a shirt and tie served as Tush's guest co-anchor.

Yet when Turner had first arranged to transmit Channel 17 by satellite, he also considered sending an all-news channel the same way. By 1978, he was ready to discuss the project with his friends and advisers. Some supported the venture, saying that the nation needed news programming superior to the hour-or-so of news the networks offered each day. Others tried to discourage him, pointing out that news shows were consistent money-losers for the networks. One day Turner called Terence McGuirk into his office and talked through the potentially ruinous $100 million scheme. By the time he had finished, Turner had finally persuaded himself to go ahead.

The Cable News Crew

Fresh from his America's Cup victory, Turner tried to assemble a winning crew for the Cable News Network (CNN). He hired Reese Schonfeld to select state-of-the-art video and computer equipment, establish bureaus, and build cooperation agreements with news gatherers around the globe. Turner and Schonfeld mulled over individuals they might want to sign, approaching Walter Cronkite, Dan Rather, Geraldo Rivera, David Frost, and Phil Donahue. As their chief Washington correspondent they picked Daniel Schorr, formerly of CBS News, who agreed to take the job after Turner persuaded the newsman that he too was serious about news. Schonfeld also recruited a group of news-show innovators who became known as Reese's Pieces: Burt Reinhardt, Ted Kavanau, and Ed Turner (who regularly had to inform people that he was not related to his boss). Later, newsman Bernard Shaw from ABC and executive Robert Wussler from CBS joined the team.

To accommodate his new venture, Turner decided to move his TBS headquarters to an old white building a few blocks away, and he asked his friend Carl Helfrich to oversee the project. Although McGuirk and Helfrich sneaked plans for tennis courts past Turner, the first CNN home was a dismal place called "the haunted house" by Dolores Woods,[29] Turner's personal assistant since 1976.

The Obstacle Course

As with so many of Ted's endeavors, there were many problems to overcome. Months before the CNN launch date of June 1, 1980, its RCA satellite, Satcom III, was lost. In order to go on the air, CNN would need a substitute transponder (an essential receiving/transmitting device) on the RCA Satcom I satellite. At a convention in San Francisco, Woods accidentally discovered that RCA did not intend to let Turner use it. She rushed to tell him about this threat to his project.

Enraged, Turner stormed into RCA's offices. He made it clear that, if he were to be ruined by RCA, he would do his best to bring that company down with him. Meeting with his team in Atlanta, he pulled a sword off a wall, dramatically brandished it aloft, and repeated his pledge. He intended to save CNN from RCA just as he had wrested the Atlanta billboard company back from Naegele in 1963. With his lawyer Tench Coxe, Turner sued RCA for the satellite space and petitioned the government; within days both sides breathed a sigh of relief when a federal order enabled CNN to have the transponder.

Money was a perpetual worry. Turner had trouble finding investors who shared his enthusiasm over an all-news cable network. He hoped to raise the necessary $1.2 million per month from cable operators who wanted to offer CNN. If he and McGuirk could not reach that goal, he was ready to use his own money to pay the difference. Although at first Turner failed to stir interest in his venture, he improved his sales pitch as the plan for CNN crystallized in his mind. Before cable operators, Turner enthusiastically described how his channel

Turner announces the beginning of CNN2. (AP/Wide World Photos)

would provide television viewers with a valuable alternative. More than any other network, CNN would attract viewers with live coverage of major news stories as they unfolded. It would offer its main news show during prime time and a sports show when other stations typically offered local news.

CNN sought revenue from advertising sales as well as cable operators. Because it was difficult to find advertisers willing to invest in programming that no one had seen, Turner had good reason to celebrate when the giant drug company Bristol-Myers signed on as the network's first advertiser, agreeing to pay $25 million over ten years to sponsor a medical news show.

The Young Lions

As word of the new enterprise spread, hundreds of applications arrived from recent college graduates who wanted to join CNN's relatively small staff. Although inexperienced, they were intelligent and ambitious—and inexpensive. CNN selected the best and the brightest of them, offering low wages for valuable experience: They did twice the amount of work they could do at overstaffed networks. One such whiz kid, Alec Nagle, worked on program schedules that would meet the different needs of viewers across different time zones. Another, Jane Maxwell, put in long hours diligently persuading local stations to enter into reciprocal agreements to trade news coverage with CNN. She told them how CNN would provide material much faster than the networks, which restricted news footage until they had used it themselves.

The atmosphere at CNN headquarters was delirious as the June 1 launch date approached. Although the newsroom was intended to be in the vanguard of computerization, technical problems forced management to install more traditional equipment for the time being. Jackhammers threatened to drown out the practice run-throughs.

Weeks before CNN was scheduled to go on air, Turner was still struggling with major money problems. When he tried to raise funds by selling his Charlotte television station for $20 million, he ran into opposition from the Charlotte Coalition, an African-American group that claimed that Turner had jeopardized his deal because the station failed to meet government quotas for hiring black employees. With Hank Aaron, Turner traveled to Charlotte to make sure that the sale could go through, succeeding by making $500,000 worth of concessions.

As the clock ticked, many media experts predicted that Ted's venture would fail miserably. Far wealthier companies, with many decades of news experience, had entered and dropped out of the competition. True to form, Turner sailed into the storm declaring, "I'm going to prove there's room for competition in this country, even if I go broke doing it."[30]

CNN on Air

On June 1, during opening-day ceremonies, as flags of Georgia, the United States, and the United Nations waved in front of his new headquarters, Turner declared that he was launching CNN

> . . . because we hope with our greater depth, and our international coverage, to make possible a better understanding of how people from different nations can live and work, and so to bring together in brotherhood and kindness and peace the people of this nation and the world.[31]

The first news items transmitted on CNN showed just how far those people had to go. The network went on the air with news of the shooting of civil rights leader Vernon Jordan in Fort Wayne, Indiana. Following items dealt with a shooting spree on an Amtrak train and gunshots that had been fired past baseball star Reggie Jackson. On a happier note, CNN reported that Turner's Braves had trounced the Los Angeles Dodgers, 9-5.

The early days of CNN were so full of mishaps that employees joked that the initials stood for Chaos News Network; outsiders called it Chicken Noodle Network because it seemed so "homemade." John Holliman delivered his agricultural report from his garden, which at first would not grow. On one occasion, the CNN audience was able to hear an angry offscreen news director swear, "I'm gonna kill him! I am going to *kill* him!"[32] Daniel Schorr himself once had to explain that his clothing had just been ignited by an exploding light bulb. Once, when Bernard Shaw was onscreen, two painters appeared in the background; on another occasion, a cleaning woman emptied his wastebasket. On his first day, weatherman Stu Siroka was hit by spinning weather-map panels. Later in his career, a technical failure caused his head to be seen floating and talking in front of a weather map.

Both CNN's staff and its news subjects had some trouble adjusting to CNN's twenty-four-hour schedule. On the first day of transmission, a correspondent was shown picking his nose. White House aides also had trouble knowing when they were on the air. Once, an assistant press secretary asked the press corps to delay the reporting of a story; he did not realize that CNN was broadcasting all of his remarks live.

Whether by luck or planning—or a combination of the two—CNN also scored some early triumphs. When, in 1980, President Jimmy Carter and presidential candidate Ronald Reagan debated but refused to let third-party candidate John Anderson participate, CNN invited him to add his comments. There were glitches as the producers worked Anderson's comments into the program using delayed transmission, but overall they succeeded. CNN scooped ABC on the fifty-four-second boxing match between Ken Norton and Gerry Cooney when it aired the one minute of footage that the cable network Home Box Office had agreed to provide. CNN also produced an award-winning piece on cases of brain cancer at a Texas chemical plant and scooped Reagan's selection of George Bush as his running mate.

Again and again, CNN's ongoing news coverage proved its worth during its first year. CNN's coverage of Hurricane Allen and a serious mishap at an Arkansas missile site demonstrated the round-the-clock network's ability to hold viewers' attention with live on-location coverage and established a precedent for covering similar stories. CNN was ready to cover events whenever and wherever they might break. It scooped, by about three minutes, coverage of the attempted assassination of Ronald Reagan on March 30, 1981, and also obtained the first footage of many of the stories surrounding that event. In April, 1981, CNN broadcast the first live footage from Cuba in two decades.

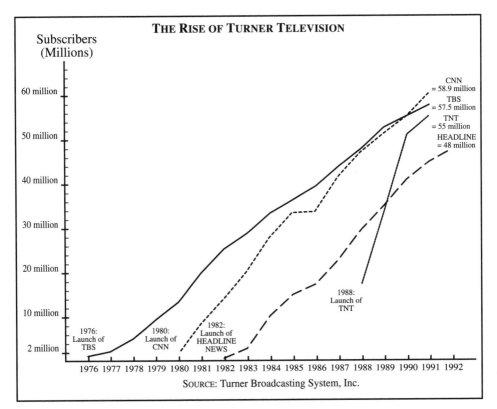

THE RISE OF TURNER TELEVISION

Subscribers (Millions)

SOURCE: Turner Broadcasting System, Inc.

Still the Underdog

Despite its successes, CNN still had to elbow its way into the network news establishment. In May, 1981, Turner and Schonfeld sued the Big Three and the office of the President of the United States because they felt that CNN was not being recognized as an equal to the networks in acquiring White House-related news. Trying to rally political support behind him and appear as the underdog in the battle, Turner also called upon Congress to investigate the networks and the film industry for "polluting the minds of our people."[33] Showing a documentary called *TV: The Moral Battleground* on CNN and the SuperStation, he called for a

> change to glorification of the good guy instead of the bad guy, change from indecency to decency, from immorality to morality, change to programming that appeals to the best in people instead of the worst.[34]

Turner had sound business reasons for fighting against the networks—especially ABC. By the time it had celebrated its first anniversary, CNN had reached its projected 6.5 million homes and exceeded expectations by adding one hundred cable operators to its original roster of seventeen. Yet, as CNN struggled to attract advertising revenue, it lost close to $2 million per month. ABC, with far greater financial strength than Turner, saw an opportunity to steal CNN's cable operators and its advertisers with a cable news operation of its own. With Westinghouse Broadcasting, ABC began to produce its own twenty-four-hour commercial cable news operation.

To fight the ABC-Westinghouse Satellite News Channels (SNC), Turner relied on two of his most valuable assets: his aggressiveness and his ability to act quickly. His near-total control of CNN enabled him to act decisively, while the large bureaucracies of ABC and Westinghouse debated their every move.

Turner's Second News Channel

Turner demonstrated his readiness to do battle when he
established a second twenty-four-hour network in a matter of
months. Correctly surmising that ABC-Westinghouse would
try to outdo TBS with a news channel that would repeat a
cycle of stories, with updates, two or three times per hour,
Turner and Schonfeld had a plan to produce one themselves.
That channel, CNN2 (later to become Headline News), began
operating on January 1, 1982, months before SNC would
unveil its version. As an added touch, on April 1, 1982, Turner
launched a twenty-four-hour CNN radio network that would
also compete with Westinghouse.

In May, 1982, SNC debuted with more than twice the
number of CNN's subscribers. Turner fought it in every arena,
including outer space, where he arranged to put CNN2 on a
satellite with five times more reach than the one used by SNC.

On a more mundane but still important level, Turner made
sure that, during newcomer SNC's early struggle, the more
seasoned CNN would be perceived as already having won the
battle for legitimacy. He was aided in his goal when CNN won
its suit against the Big Three and the President. Now CNN
would be like a Fourth Network at the White House, equal to
the Big Three in obtaining access to news stories there. CNN
continued to prove its worth with captivating coverage from
trouble spots such as El Salvador and landmark programs such
as *Moscow Live*, a news show based in the United States and
the Soviet Union.

The King of Cable News

Turner himself grew in prominence during this period. He
even met with Cuban leader Fidel Castro, who appeared
unable to resist "pirating" CNN transmissions for his own use.
"When there's trouble in the world," the Cuban leader said, "I
turn to CNN." "He was very nice to me," Turner recalled, "and

The ups and downs of team ownership: The Atlanta Hawks won this 1983 NBA play-off against Boston's Celtics 95-93. (AP/Wide World Photos)

I certainly think he'd like to have good relations with the United States. He said it's hard to understand that America can trade with Russia and not trade with them. . . . I told him, 'Well, you're always saying bad things about us. Ease up a bit.'"[35]

As much as advertisers and cable operators joined with Castro in their respect for Turner and CNN, they used the news war to win bargains for themselves. It was in this financial arena that Turner was most vulnerable: Only ABC-Westinghouse could afford to transmit to cable operators free-of-charge. Turner tried to rally cable operators behind him, pointing out that he was their longtime ally against the Big Three. He offered package deals that were consistently topped by ABC-Westinghouse, which turned out to be willing to *pay* cable operators for carrying SNC. ABC-Westinghouse used its monetary clout in other ways: Just as CNN had lured personnel away from the Big Three, SNC hired CNN employees away from Turner.

Both ABC-Westinghouse and Turner were losing large amounts of money as the battle mounted. As he had done in the past, Turner gambled on wearing down his opponent with tenacity. To outlast his rival, he looked for ways to control costs. He replaced Schonfeld, who had wisely invested large amounts of money in launching CNN, with Burt Reinhardt, who would now manage the network's budget with more austerity. Turner also took out a large loan and sold some unprofitable properties.

When, at the end of 1982, SNC sales forces took time off, Turner saw his golden opportunity. CNN2 sales representatives offered to pay cable operators who signed up for both CNN channels. Turner also put his lawyer Tench Coxe on the offensive, triggering a suit against SNC interests for conspiring against his news channels. Like the satellite transponder suit he had filed against RCA, this legal battle threatened to drive ABC-Westinghouse's losses too high. The strategy paid off: In 1983, Turner successfully offered $25 million for SNC and its several million subscribers. Signing off on October 27, the anchorman said, "And now, Ted buddy, it's in your hands!"[36] Turner soon shut SNC down.

Turner's conquest over SNC led *Newsweek* to dub him the "King of Cable News." CNN had debuted in Australia, Canada, and Japan. By 1984, The Media Institute, a research foundation, found that CNN outperformed its broadcast competition, offering "business and economic reporting . . . more balanced and less sensational than that of the networks."[37] There were still mishaps, but Turner had clearly steered CNN into calmer waters. In 1985, CNN finally overcame its years of financial losses by posting a net income of more than $20 million.

Chapter 7

Shifting Winds

With his successful SuperStation and cable news network, Turner had many reasons to be pleased by the mid-1980's. Even the Atlanta Braves, which continued to lose money, had briefly turned around and reached the playoffs in 1982. But all was not well.

Back in 1977, when he was competing in the America's Cup, Turner had told Roger Vaughan how he organized his life. "My priorities are in order. I've never had any problems with priorities. Mine are sailing, business, and family, in that order."[38] By 1986, Turner's priorities had come back to haunt him. Rushing from business meeting to sailing event to baseball game to basketball game to business meeting had left him little time for his family.

Turner's private life suggested that, as far as his personal conduct was concerned, he was alarmingly like his father. Jimmy Brown, still a family employee after forty years, worried that Turner might similarly work himself into an early grave. Turner's mother Florence complained that she saw her son only as he rushed between appointments. His children found him an intimidating, unsympathetic father who rarely had time for them. "If he caught you crying, that was the worst thing you could do," remembered his son Teddy.[39]

Turner's wife Janie—herself running out of patience with him—finally persuaded her husband to seek psychiatric help. Over the following years, Ted underwent counseling and drug treatment to help moderate his behavior. Long aware that his painful childhood experiences and the example set by his parents' behavior somehow shaped his own behavior as an

France's President François Mitterrand meets Turner and wife Janie at the French embassy in Moscow in 1986. (AP/Wide World Photos)

adult, he now devoted serious effort to analyzing their effects and improving himself. He even stopped chewing tobacco and smoking cigars.

Ted and Janie's efforts did not, however, prevent their marriage from falling apart. As Ted spent more time in the company of another woman, J. J. Ebaugh, he and Janie separated in 1986, and they were finally divorced in 1988. Their settlement required him to provide Janie with $40 million.

The Goodwill Games

Besides seeking self-improvement, Turner devoted more effort to improving the world—even when it cost him a lot of money. Although he had previously expressed an interest in world affairs, as head of CNN and the SuperStation he was now in a position to know more and do more about his concerns than most people. In 1982, the SuperStation entered into a contract with the Cousteau Society to air original programming covering Jacques Cousteau's explorations. In following years, Turner negotiated a programming exchange agreement with the Soviet Union, established the Turner Tomorrow Awards (to honor the best fiction manuscript with a positive message about Earth's future), and formed the Better World Society to make television programs supporting limited population growth, environmental preservation, and an end to the nuclear arms race. In addition to Jimmy Carter, the members of the society's international board included prominent figures from the Soviet Union, Nigeria, and Norway, among other nations. Its documentaries appeared on TBS channels.

Turner also promoted himself as an emissary of world peace by launching the Goodwill Games. After the Soviet Union invaded Afghanistan in 1979, the Cold War between the United States and the Soviet Union had escalated to the point where the two nations refused to participate in the Olympic Games hosted in each other's countries. Turner, who had long cast an envious eye on television coverage of the Summer Olympic Games, decided to organize an event where athletes from the two superpowers could again compete—and be seen on his SuperStation.

The first Goodwill Games began at Moscow's Lenin Stadium in July, 1986. For two weeks, thousands of athletes from seventy countries competed against one another in the name of international friendship. Track-and-field superstar Jackie Joyner set a world record in the heptathlon. The United States women's basketball team made an impressive showing, as did hurdler Edwin Moses and Soviet pole-vaulter Sergei Bubka.

There were some blemishes, however. The Soviet Union

prevented the participation of Israel and South Korea. President Ronald Reagan barred twelve members of the United States military from competing. Soviet officials tampered with track events to give an advantage to their country's participants. Finally, the television coverage—during which Turner served as commentator for the yachting competition—was disappointing, attracting only a small share of the viewing audience.

A Financial Crisis

Turner gained much publicity staging the Goodwill Games, but he lost approximately $26 million in the process. Along with his expensive divorce settlement, other business losses during the same period made many experts suspect that the media maverick had finally reached the end of his winning streak.

Throughout his career, Ted had always seemed to thrive in the fiercely competitive media business, building radio and television enterprises despite opposition from rivals. Some of his business dealings in the mid-1980's, however, had many wondering whether he had lost his touch. In 1983, for example, he tried to compete against MTV with Night Tracks, a block of programs that offered a broader range of music. In 1985, he abandoned the venture, allowing MTV to buy its assets.

Also in 1985, Turner tried to buy CBS. Resisting his attempt to buy 67 percent of the network, CBS bought back 20 percent of its stock, placing itself in dangerous financial straits. Observers did not know whether to call Turner a failure for not completing the acquisition or a success for damaging a rival network.

By the end of the year, however, most were ready to say that Turner had made a serious mistake. His next major business venture was the purchase of the debt-ridden

MGM/UA Entertainment Company from Kirk Kerkorian.
Knowing of Turner's interest in owning the MGM film library,
which included *Gone with the Wind* and *The Wizard of Oz*,
Kerkorian offered him the company for $1.4 billion—a
staggering amount, thought to exceed the actual worth of the
property by about $500 million. Turner, who quickly agreed to
the deal, soon found himself scrambling to raise the payments
necessary to keep his new acquisition. Having bitten off more
than he could chew, he finally sold back most of the purchase
to Kerkorian, at a loss. Hollywood analysts almost
unanimously concluded that Turner had more than met his
match in Kerkorian.

On the Comeback Trail

To minimize his losses from the MGM acquisition, Ted
accepted an offer from a consortium of cable operators. This
group, which had benefited in the past from Ted's pioneering
efforts, agreed to provide more than $562 million in exchange
for a major share of TBS, as well as almost half the seats on its
board of directors. Rather than take control of Ted's company,
the cable operators showed faith in his business abilities by
giving him some time to make TBS successful again.

Ted did not disappoint them. In 1988, when both the
SuperStation and CNN first reached 50 percent of American
television households, he launched enterprises such as World
Championship Wrestling, Inc., and the entertainment-oriented
Turner Network Television (TNT), which used the movies in
the newly acquired MGM film library as its programming
core. Debuting in almost twenty million homes, it was the
largest network launch in the history of cable television.

To attract viewers and advertisers to the channel, Turner
decided to *colorize* some of the best-known movies in his
collection. Colorization is a technique used to make
black-and-white films look as if they had been shot in color.

Shocked that he would tamper with the subtly shaded look of black-and-white film classics such as *Casablanca*, prominent directors such as Woody Allen and Steven Spielberg appeared before Congress to protest the practice, but Turner proceeded anyway. The controversy caught the public's interest and put

1988: Turner raises hands with athletes Jackie Joyner-Kersee and Edwin Moses as they announce, via satellite link from Los Angeles, an agreement with Russia to extend the Goodwill Games into 1994 and 1998. (AP/Wide World Photos)

Turner in a position of being both a villain and a hero among film lovers: Criticized by some for demeaning black-and-white films with colorization, he was praised by others for producing beautifully restored black-and-white copies in the process. He also supervised excellent restorations of color films such as *The Wizard of Oz* and *Gone with the Wind*, one of his favorites. Although colorization did not reap vast financial returns for Turner, his risky investment in the MGM film library seemed vindicated by TNT's popularity: It was the fastest-growing cable network ever.

Crisis News Network

Turner's determination to save TBS paid off: In 1990, boosted by the international success of CNN and Headline News, the company earned a profit for the first time since 1985. The second Goodwill Games lost $44 million, but Turner took consolation in TNT's rapid growth and CNN's ascent to world prominence. No longer a "down-and-dirty" operation based in a decrepit old building, CNN had blossomed into an award-winning news organization that was housed, along with Headline News and CNN Radio, in state-of-the-art facilities at TBS headquarters in Atlanta's plush CNN Center.

Because CNN's proudest moments generally consisted of its coverage of the world's most dramatic news stories, some jokingly began to call it "Crisis News Network." In 1986, anxious viewers tuned in to watch CNN coverage of the explosion of the *Challenger* space shuttle and the United States' attack on Libya. CNN later won Peabody Awards—a high honor in broadcasting—for its coverage of the 1987 stock market crash and the 1989 Tiananmen Square massacre. Other major news events covered by CNN included the fall of the Berlin Wall (1989), the United States' invasion of Panama (1989), and the release of South African anti-apartheid leader Nelson Mandela (1990). Never before had the television screen provided such a wide window on world events.

Chapter 8

Captain Planet

World leaders, rival news organizations, and ordinary citizens explored the global village through the CNN camera lenses. Those who witnessed CNN's Tiananmen Square coverage would never forget the inspiring image of a lone man attempting to discourage the approach of tanks, or the unsettling feeling as Chinese government officials terminated the network's transmission. Sadly, besides documenting the violent suppression of peaceful pro-democracy demonstrators in the People's Republic of China, CNN's coverage may also have served another, harmful purpose: It was probably used by the Chinese government to identify and further persecute the youthful protestors.

CNN at War

CNN's role in world affairs became even more prominent after Iraq's Saddam Hussein ordered the invasion of Kuwait in the summer of 1990. Over the following months, leaders such as Turkish President Turgut Ozal used CNN to keep track of the world's attempts to persuade Hussein to withdraw his forces before mid-January, when the United Nations coalition was authorized to use military force.

As the deadline approached and negotiations stalled, U.S. officials urged their fellow citizens, including members of the press, to leave Iraq. Despite this warning, a CNN team remained. On January 15 in Iraq, Turner called his reporting team in Baghdad to offer them encouragement. Realizing how important CNN had become as a diplomatic tool, he expressed some hope that his reporters might somehow represent a last

chance for peace. In his book *Live from Baghdad,* producer
Robert Wiener recalled him saying:

> I'm afraid it's too late for [a chance at a peaceful settlement], but if
> there is, it might come through us. . . . Hell, both sides aren't talkin'
> to each other, but they're talkin' to CNN. We have a major
> responsibility.[40]

Turner's fears were well founded. On the evening of
January 16, the largest prime-time audience in cable
history—10.8 million households—turned on CNN and saw
the skies of Baghdad light up as U.N. coalition forces began
bombardment. Over the following weeks, the world continued
to watch the war unfold. Live coverage enabled viewers
everywhere to share the anxiety of a panic-stricken reporter in
Israel frantically struggling to put on a gas mask, and the
jittery fear of a reporter in Saudi Arabia running to shelter
himself in anticipation of a missile strike.

By the end of the conflict, viewers had also seen reporter
Peter Arnett cover scenes of destruction in Iraq. Many U.S.
citizens complained that such reporting, tightly controlled by
Hussein, constituted Iraqi propaganda. In an interview with
David Frost, Turner defended such reporting by citing CNN's
global character:

> We try to present the facts as they are, not from a U.S. perspective but
> from a human perspective. . . . You know. . . I believe that our
> humanity supersedes our nationalism.[41]

Man of the Year

In 1991, the increasingly important role of CNN, which also
gripped viewers with extensive coverage of the ascent of
Russian leader Boris Yeltsin in August, earned Turner the
designation of *Time* magazine's Man of the Year, for
"influencing the dynamic of events and turning viewers in 150

countries into instant witnesses of history."[42]

Turner had certainly come a long way in the twenty-one years since he had acquired his tiny UHF station. Having survived numerous setbacks, he looked virtually indestructible as a businessman. TBS continued its resurgence, reporting record income and revenues. In another kind of comeback, the Atlanta Braves came from behind to win the 1991 National League Pennant, only losing to the Minnesota Twins in the seventh game of a well-played World Series. He acquired the entertainment assets of the giant cartoon producer Hanna-Barbera in December. Although he disbanded the Better World Society, he established the Turner Family Foundation to donate money to charitable causes, and he received the Spirit of America prize from People for the American Way.

May 17, 1990: Turner is joined by seven-foot, seven-inch Argentine wrestler Jorge Gonzales, who was signed to Turner's cable wrestling network. (AP/Wide World Photos)

A Third Marriage

Also in 1991, Ted married Jane Fonda, after an intense courtship that included a cruise of the Greek islands with Peter Dames (the friend from Brown University who, years before, had introduced Turner to Janie). The pair shared common interests and admiration for each other. Together, they elected to stop drinking alcohol. Before and during their marriage, they attended events in support of environmental causes, including the 1992 Earth Summit in Brazil.

Early in the marriage, Turner seemed to be succeeding in his efforts to become a better husband than he had been in the past. "He's a dream man," Fonda told newswoman Maria Shriver in a television interview.[43] Perhaps inspired by his wife, Ted decided to appear in *The Killer Angels*, an original TNT television movie about the Battle of Gettysburg.

Testing Television's Bounds

Restless as ever, Ted busied himself overseeing many other projects in 1992, continuing his search for new ways to use television technology in the twenty-first century. In January, TBS introduced the Checkout Channel, which displays news and advertisements on television monitors seen by shoppers waiting in supermarket checkout lines. In the summer, TBS and the McDonald's Corporation conducted an eight-week test of "McDTV," a channel seen in McDonald's restaurants. In October, after winning a special Emmy Award for his contributions to the television industry, he launched the Cartoon Channel, another twenty-four-hour network, showcasing the animated features that TBS had acquired with the MGM and Hanna-Barbera libraries. (Also among Turner's holdings is an original animated series tracing the adventures of the superhero Captain Planet, who fights to protect earth's environment.) In the planning stage was the Airport Channel, which would deliver live news programming to airline terminals. Another ambitious project was the production of a history of Native American peoples in both book and video formats.

Global Legacy

A look at Ted Turner's accomplishments makes one thing clear: His willingness to fight for victory as long as he can see a chance for success serves as an example to anyone embarking on a business, sports, or personal venture. "I just love it when people say I can't do something," he has said:

> There's nothing that makes me feel better, because all my life people have said I wasn't going to make it. . . . The secret of my success is this: Every time, I tried to go as far as I could. When I climbed the hills, I saw the mountains. Then I started climbing the mountains.[44]

Over four decades, Turner has reached the summits of many of those mountains. In realizing his ambitions, he has enabled others to find fulfillment as well. Ventures such as CNN created opportunities for experienced reporters as well as the talented college graduates who put in long, difficult hours during the network's early years. As the leader of the Goodwill Games, he has enabled athletes from quarreling nations to meet and compete, fostering an environment of international understanding.

As a cable pioneer, Ted Turner helped liberate the television industry from years of Big Three domination. As a noted yachtsman, he led crew members to victory again and again. As a broadcaster and owner of the Braves and the Hawks, he enlivened leisure time in Atlanta and the rest of the country, and gave a publicist like Bob Hope and a retired player like Hank Aaron an opportunity to demonstrate the full range of their abilities. Even though the Braves lost a second consecutive World Series in 1992 to the Toronto Blue Jays, the team continued to demonstrate the same kind of tenacity that

George Bennett

enabled its owner to prevail in many different arenas.

Some of Ted Turner's achievements are harder to evaluate. By founding an international all-news television network, he has helped realize Marshall McLuhan's vision of a global village, enabling people to learn more about themselves and their world through the electronic media. It remains to be seen, however, if such knowledge will prove as beneficial as Turner would like. Coverage of the Tiananmen Square protest did not, for example, prevent the government of the People's Republic of China from cracking down on the protestors.

People have wondered whether Ted Turner will run for the office of President of the United States or even receive a Nobel Prize. Certainly, he has stated his desire to make a difference in world affairs: "Someday I'm going to be the first person in the history of the world to be able to talk to everyone," he has declared. "I'll be able to talk to all the world's leaders and bring peace to the world through television."[45]

Although Ted Turner's creation of CNN has drastically affected the way people understand the world, it is as a husband, father, and world citizen that Turner may have achieved what could be anybody's greatest accomplishment: learning to confront his personal flaws and improve himself. Once far more concerned with indulging his business and sporting interests than with building a happy family, he learned the importance of treating his wife and children with love, tenderness, and consideration. Having jeopardized his health with his use of tobacco and alcohol, he learned to enjoy life without those vices. Once noted for making bigoted and sexist remarks, he became an outspoken champion of humanitarian and environmental causes.

Though still an aggressive entrepreneur, he has possibly even surprised even himself by discovering the pleasures of life's more tranquil moments. In a 1991 interview with David Frost, Turner reflected:

I've made a number of transitions in my life, one of them [to] being relatively . . . secure. . . . I've become more of a progressive over the last fifteen years . . . as I've been exposed to more things. I've gone from a rampant nationalist to a rampant internationalist. I've gone from someone that was in the billboard business to someone that was in the television business, someone that was racing sailboats to . . . fly fishing. That's a totally different thing. Racing a sailboat at sea is the most frenetic and hectic thing you can do. And fishing alone on a stream, on a quiet stream for trout with a fly rod is the most solitary, quiet and . . . it's almost a Zen experience. It's totally, totally different.[46]

For Ted Turner, a man raised to be fiercely combative, perhaps the greatest accomplishment has been achieving that measure of inner peace.

The Turner Empire

Property	Date	Significance
Turner Advertising Company	1963	The company thrives under Turner's leadership
Channel 17	1970-1976	Turner turns an unprofitable local station into a nationally successful superstation
Atlanta Braves	1976	Turner secures sports programming as well as a vehicle for self-promotion
America's Cup	1977	Turner's yachting career reaches its zenith as he defends the cup in four straight victories
Cable News Network (CNN) Headline News (CNN2)	1980-1982	Turner creates the first all-news cable television networks
Goodwill Games and Better World Society	1985	Turner sponsors humanitarian projects
MGM film and television library	1986	Turner acquires valuable television programming material
Turner Network Television	1988	Turner creates a television network to showcase his MGM properties.
Cartoon Network	1992	Turner launches his fifth cable television network.

Time Line

1938   Robert Edward (Ted) Turner III is born in Cincinnati, Ohio, on November 19.

1944   Turner attends a Cincinnati boarding school.

1948   Turner attends a military academy near Atlanta.

1950   Turner begins studies at The McCallie School, a military academy in Chattanooga, Tennessee.

1956   Turner enters Brown University.

1958   Turner's sister Mary Jane dies.

1960   Turner becomes general manager of the Turner Advertising Company branch in Macon, Georgia.

1963   Turner's father commits suicide. Turner becomes president and chief operating officer of Turner Advertising Company.

1964   Turner marries Janie Smith, his second wife.

1970   Turner Communications Group acquires Atlanta's UHF Channel 17, renaming it WTCG.
        Turner is named Yachtsman of the Year.

1973   Turner is named Yachtsman of the Year for the second time.

1974   Turner loses the America's Cup competition.

1976   Turner acquires the Atlanta Braves baseball team.
        Using satellite and cable technology, Turner converts WTCG into a SuperStation available nationwide.

1977   Turner purchases a controlling interest in the Atlanta Hawks basketball team.
        Turner wins the America's Cup on the yacht *Courageous* and earns Yachtsman of the Year designation an unprecedented third time.

1979   Turner wins Great Britain's Fastnet competition and receives Yachtsman of the Year title a fourth time.

Turner Communications Group is renamed Turner Broadcasting System, Inc. (TBS). WTCG becomes WTBS.

1980   Turner establishes Cable News Network (CNN).

1982   Turner launches CNN2 (soon to be known as Headline News) and the twenty-four-hour all-news CNN Radio.

WTBS and The Cousteau Society agree to air original programming.

CNN initiates transmissions to Japan.

The Atlanta Braves reach the playoffs.

1983   Turner Educational Services is formed to bring TBS programming into schools.

CNN buys out competitor Satellite News Channels and begins transmission to Australia.

Turner launches Night Tracks and receives the Distinguished Alumnus Award from McCallie.

1984   CNN wins the Peabody Award for Excellence in Programming and begins transmissions to Canada.

1985   Headline News is launched in Canada.

CNN International is launched in Europe.

Night Tracks is bought out by MTV.

Turner offers $5.4 billion for the CBS television network but does not complete the purchase.

Turner forms the Better World Society.

1986   After acquiring MGM/UA Entertainment Company for more than $1.2 billion in borrowed money, TBS sells back portions for almost $800 million. Left with the MGM film and television library, Turner creates the Turner Entertainment Company (TEC) to manage it.

Turner mounts the Goodwill Games in Moscow at a cost of $26 million.

Turner leaves Janie to live with J. J. Ebaugh.

1987   CNN begins transmission to the People's Republic of China.

A consortium of cable investors purchases 36 percent of TBS.

1988 CNN and TBS reach 50 percent of American television households.

CNN wins the Peabody Award for coverage of the 1987 stock market crash and begins producing Spanish-language newscasts for Telemundo Network.

Turner Network Television (TNT) debuts.

TBS forms World Championship Wrestling, Inc.

Turner and Janie are divorced.

1989 TNT's *The Making of a Legend: Gone with the Wind* wins the Peabody Award.

Turner is awarded an honorary degree by Brown University.

1990 CNN wins a third Peabody Award, for coverage of the student uprising in the People's Republic of China.

The second Goodwill Games are held in Seattle.

TBS, TCI Sports Inc., and Scripps Howard Productions establish the regional sports network SportSouth.

Turner networks win five news and documentary Emmy Awards.

TNT reaches 50 million subscribers.

1991 On January 16, CNN reaches a record 10.8 million households with its coverage of the Persian Gulf War.

TBS reports an annual net profit for the first time since 1985.

The Better World Society folds; Turner establishes the Turner Family Foundation and receives the Spirit of Liberty prize from People for the American Way.

The Atlanta Braves win the National League pennant.

Turner acquires the entertainment assets of Hanna-Barbera.

Turner marries Jane Fonda.

Time magazine anoints Turner Man of the Year.

1992 TBS reports record revenues and net income for 1991.

The Checkout Channel appears in some supermarkets.

1992   The Atlanta Braves win a second consecutive National League pennant.

Turner receives a special Emmy Award for contributions to the television industry.

The Cartoon Network debuts.

Notes

Full bibliographic information is listed in the Bibliography and Media Resources.

1. Vaughan, *Mouth*, p. 111.
2. "Ted Turner at The McCallie School," press release, May, 1992.
3. Hope, pp.140-141.
4. Vaughan, *Gesture*, pp. 22-23.
5. Whittemore, p. 16.
6. Hope, p. 68.
7. Hope, p. 68.
8. Williams, p. 172.
9. Whittemore, p. 26.
10. Aaron, p. 416.
11. Hope, p. 113.
12. Hope. p. 81.
13. Hope, p. 81.
14. Vaughan, *Mouth*, p. 121.
15. "A New Look for the Old Ball Game," *Time*, vol. 107, no. 17 (April 26, 1976).
16. Hope, p. 150.
17. Vaughan, *Mouth*, p. 36.
18. Conner, p. 41.
19. Vaughan, *Mouth*, p. xvii.
20. McCormick, Herb, "Dennis Speaks," *Sailing World*, vol. 31, no. 2 (February, 1992).
21. "A New Look for the Old Ball Game," *Time*, vol. 107, no. 17 (April 26, 1976).
22. Whittemore, p. 37.
23. Vaughan, *Mouth*, p. 12.
24. Turner and Jobson, p. 22.
25. Vaughan, *Mouth*, p. 77.
26. Vaughan, *Mouth*, pp. 21-27.

27. The incident is described in both Vaughan, *Mouth*, pp. 206-207, and Williams, pp. 152-153.
28. Williams, p. 16.
29. Whittemore, p. 75.
30. Williams, p. 15.
31. Williams, p. 5.
32. Whittemore, p. 154.
33. Whittemore, p. 197.
34. Whittemore, p. 197.
35. Whittemore, p. 233.
36. Whittemore, p. 257.
37. The Media Institute, *CNN versus the Networks: Is More News Better News?*, with a foreword by Patrick D. Maines. Washington, D.C.: The Media Institute, 1984, p. x.
38. Vaughan, *Mouth*, pp. 127-128.
39. Smith, Gary. "What Makes Turner Run?" *Sports Illustrated* 64, no. 25 (June 23, 1986).
40. *Live from Baghdad: Gathering News at Ground Zero.* New York: Doubleday, 1992, p. 253.
41. David Paradine Television. *Talking with David Frost*, aired October 25, 1991.
42. *Time*, "Prince of the Global Village," January 6, 1992.
43. *First Person with Maria Shriver*, aired May 6, 1992.
44. Whittemore, p. 14.
45. Hope, p. 143.
46. David Paradine Television. *Talking with David Frost*, aired October 25, 1991.

Glossary

Advertising: An industry in which a client purchases media space (such as billboards or broadcast time) for the dissemination of a business message.

Advertising revenue: Money received in exchange for advertising space. In general, advertising revenue increases with audience size and purchasing power.

Affiliate: A television station, usually independent, that has agreed to carry programs of a particular network.

America's Cup: An international yachting competition, held every three years, in which the previous winner "defends" the trophy against a "challenger" over a series of races.

Billboard: An advertising space along a roadway. Outdoor advertising firms earn revenue from clients who pay to put their messages on billboards.

Broadcasting: A field in which radio and television transmissions are intended for reception by the general public.

Cable operator: A company that transmits television signals to subscribers
via cable.

Cable television: An industry based on transmitting television signals into homes via cable.

Entrepreneur: A person responsible for devising and realizing a business enterprise.

Global village: Canadian media theorist Marshall McLuhan's term for the modern world, in which electronic media act as extensions of the human senses.

Mass communication: The sending of a message or messages to a large number of people.

Mass media: The industries (such as publishing and broadcasting) that provide vehicles for mass communication, or the vehicles (such as books, films, or television) themselves.

Network: A group of broadcasting stations offering the same programs. Over the course of television history, ABC, CBS, and NBC established themselves as the Big Three networks, dominating television programming in the United States. Beginning in the 1970's, alternatives such as cable television reduced the Big Three's share of the television viewing audience.

News feed: Footage of current events provided to news shows for presentation in their broadcasts.

Scoop (*verb*): To report a news story first.

Superstation: An independent station that uses satellite technology to send its signal nationwide.

Tactician: In yachting, the crew member who advises the skipper concerning strategy.

Telecommunications: The transmission and reception of signals by electromagnetic means, using television, radio, telephone, computer, or satellite technology or a combination of these technologies.

UHF: An acronym for "ultra high frequency," the television frequency band used for channels 14 through 83 in North America. Until the advent of cable, this band was hard to receive and dominated by independent stations. VHF, "very high frequency," is used for channels 2 through 13.

Bibliography

Aaron, Hank, with Lonnie Wheeler. *I Had a Hammer*. New York: HarperPaperbacks, 1992. An admiring associate of Turner, baseball legend Aaron provides some insight into the tycoon's business dealings, especially with regard to racial issues. Of special interest are the lgendary slugger's accounts of meetings between Turner and Jesse Jackson.

Blair, Gwenda. "Once More, with Cheek." *Business Month* 132, no. 1 (July/August, 1988). A succinct history of TBS prior to TNT's debut, this article offers clearly written summaries of some of Turner's riskiest business ventures.

Conner, Dennis. *No Excuse to Lose: Winning Yacht Races with Dennis Conner*. New York: W. W. Norton, 1978. The champion yachtsman offers views of Turner as captain and competitor. This volume, which includes a chapter on sailing *Mariner* in the 1974 America's Cup race, concludes by grouping Turner with such leading skippers as Lowell North and Ted Hood.

Dawson, Greg. "Ted Turner." *American Film* 14 (January/February, 1989). Turner is outspoken in an interview revolving around his film and video interests. Among the subjects covered are his controversial use of film colorization and the relative artistic merits of the television series *Gilligan's Island* and the film classic *Citizen Kane*.

Hope, Bob. *We Could've Finished Last Without You: An Irreverent Look at the Atlanta Braves, the Losingest Team in Baseball for the Past Twenty-five Years*. Atlanta: Longstreet Press, 1991. Former Atlanta Braves publicist Bob Hope (not the comedian) helped bring notoriety to the team and its owner, Ted Turner, in the late 1970's. His entertaining memoir details many of his and Turner's promotional exploits.

Lanham, Julia. "The Greening of Ted Turner." *The Humanist* 34, no. 6 (November/December, 1989). This article emphasizes the environmental and humanitarian concerns of Turner, who was

designated the 1990 Humanist of the Year by the American
Humanist Association.

Painton, Priscilla. "The Taming of Ted Turner." *Time* 134, no. 1
(January 6, 1992). The centerpiece of *Time*'s tribute to Turner as
Man of the Year, this cover story is accompanied by three
complementary features: "Prince of the Global Village" explains
why the editors selected Turner as the individual with the most
impact on the news in 1991; "History As It Happens" discusses
the importance of Turner's news channels; and "Inside the World
of CNN" examines the daily operations of Cable News Network.

Smith, Gary. "What Makes Turner Run?" *Sports Illustrated* 64, no.
25 (June 23, 1986). Smith's portrait of Turner on the eve of the
first Goodwill Games kicked off *Sports Illustrated*'s coverage of
the competition. The author speculates on the psychological
origins of Turner's great ambition.

Stutz, Bruce. "Ted Turner Turns It On." *Audubon* 93, no. 6
(November/December, 1991). Months before the 1992 Earth
Summit in Brazil, Turner spoke to an environmental reporter
about such global issues as overpopulation, urban development,
and dwindling resources. The resulting interview captures his
erratic conversational style as well as his wide range of opinions.

Turner, Ted, and Gary Jobson. *The Racing Edge*. New York: Simon
& Schuster, 1979. Shortly after their America's Cup victory,
Turner and Jobson offer sailing pointers in a heavily illustrated
volume. Also included are a glossary of sailing terms and an
interview in which Jobson asks Turner questions about his
competitive attitude. This book is of particular interest to readers
with sailing experience.

Vaughan, Roger. *The Grand Gesture: Ted Turner, Mariner and the
America's Cup*. Boston: Little, Brown, 1975. Vaughan, a
yachtsman and onetime classmate of Turner at Brown University,
recounts the 1974 America's Cup competition in text and
photographs.

_____. *Ted Turner: The Man Behind the Mouth*. New York:
Sail Books/Norton, 1978. Vaughan follows Turner's comeback
from loss to triumph at the 1977 America's Cup competition. Not

surprisingly, this book captures the yachting maverick at his most dashing.

Waters, Harry F. "Ted Turner Tackles TV News." *Newsweek* 95, no. 24 (June 16, 1980). Written on the occasion of CNN's debut, this article captures Turner's momentum as he embarks on a new venture. It includes fifteen photographs of the tycoon at various points in his life.

Whittemore, Hank. *CNN: The Inside Story.* New York: Little, Brown, 1990. Whittemore profiles Turner and the other personalities behind the creation of the first all-news network, conveying an impression of the chemistry behind one of Turner's most successful team enterprises.

Williams, Christian. *Lead, Follow, or Get Out of the Way.* New York: Times Books, 1981. This biography of Turner features a detailed description of the Fastnet race by a writer who, as a member of Turner's crew, personally weathered its dangerous winds and waves.

Media Resources

CBS News (Drew Phillips, segment producer). "Ted Turner." Segment of *60 Minutes* with Harry Reasoner. Originally aired April 22, 1979. Transcript available for purchase from Burrell's Transcripts, P.O. Box 7, Livingston, N.J. 07039. Reasoner touches on Turner's varied activities during one of the entrepreneur's most exciting periods.

CBS News (Jan Legnito, segment producer). "Ted Turner." Segment of *60 Minutes* with Diane Sawyer. Originally aired April 20, 1986. Transcript available for purchase from Burrell's Transcripts, P.O. Box 7, Livingston, N.J. 07039. Sawyer focuses on the failed CBS takeover bid as well as Turner's global philosophy.

David Paradine Television (David Frost and John Florescu, executive producers). "Ted Turner." Episode of *Talking with David Frost*. Originally aired October 25, 1991. Transcript available from PBS Video Transcripts, 1535 Grant St., Denver, Colo. 80203. Videotape available from PBS Video, P.O. Box 791, Alexandria, Va. Two games into the 1991 World Series, Turner expounds on a wide array of subjects.

National Broadcasting Company (Michael Rourke, segment producer). "Ted Turner." Segment of *First Person with Maria Shriver*. Originally aired May 6, 1992. Transcript available from NBC News Transcripts, P.O. Box 7, Livingston, N.J. 07039. This profile reveals Turner's capacity to be a difficult interview subject, intimidating Shriver as he aggressively twists her questions to his advantage.

Offshore Productions. *America's Cup 1974: The Grandest Prize*. 1974. Available from Mystic Seaport Museum, Film-Video Archives, P.O. Box 6000, 50 Greenmanville Ave., Mystic, Conn. 06355-0990. Volume 4 in the Thomas J. Lipton America's Cup Yachting Series, this tape captures the intense competition between Turner, Ted Hood, and Dennis Conner as they vied to defend the Cup against the Australian challenger.

Offshore Productions. *America's Cup 1977: The Best Defense* and *America's Cup 1980: Freedom*. 1977 and 1980. Available from Mystic Seaport Museum, Film-Video Archives, P.O. Box 6000, 50 Greenmanville Ave., Mystic, Conn. 06355-0990. Volume 5 in the Lipton series, this combined program follows Turner's rise and fall at the America's Cup competition, as Conner ushers in a new era of ultra-expensive and madly competitive America's Cup racing.

INDEX